S0-BYX-292

BAD PEOPLE
IN HISTORY

Roland C. Barker

Gramercy Books
New York

This 2001 edition is published by Gramercy Books™, an imprint of
Random House Value Publishing, Inc., 280 Park Avenue, New York, N.Y. 10017.

Gramercy Books™ and design are trademarks of Random House Value Publishing, Inc.

Random House
New York • Toronto • London • Sydney • Auckland
http://www.randomhouse.com/

Designed by Robert Yaffe

Printed and bound in the United States of America

On the cover: Adolph Hitler (Hulton Getty/Liaison Agency), Al Capone (Hulton Getty/Liaison Agency), Rasputin played by Conrad Veidt (Hulton Getty/Liaison Agency)

Library of Congress Cataloging-in-Publication Data

Barker, Roland C.
    Bad people in history / Roland C. Barker.
        p. cm.
    ISBN 0-517-16311-X
    1. Kings and rulers—History. 2. Heads of state—History. 3. Dictators—History.
  4. Brigands and robbers—History. 5. Mass murderers—History. I. Title.

  D107 .B34 2001
  909'.0092'2–dc21

                                                                        00-057795

9 8 7 6 5 4 3 2 1

BAD PEOPLE
IN HISTORY

A

IDI AMIN   Dictator of Uganda in the 1970s who expelled all 70,000 Ugandan Asians, many Israelis, seized foreign-owned businesses, and ordered the killing of an estimated 300,000 people. Amin was over-thrown in 1979 and since then has lived in exile in Saudi Arabia.

POPE ALEXANDER VI   The most decadent of the Renaissance popes, Rodrigo Borgia—the leading figure of the famous Borgia family—conducted a regime of nepotism, greed, ruthlessness, murder, and unbridled sensuality. He fathered several illegitimate children, including the notorious Lucretia and Cesare, with various mistresses. He is best known for the torture and execution in 1498 of the Florentine preacher Savonarola who had challenged the papal corruption. He died after drinking poison that he had prepared for an enemy.

ALBERT ANASTASIA   Known as the "Lord High Executioner" of Murder, Inc., the crime syndicate that was paid to kill anyone who got in the way of the big bosses like Al Capone, Frank Costello, and Lucky Luciano. His ruthless brutality eventually got him the top seat in what was to become the Gambino family, which he ruled with familiar terror and violence. Also known as the "Mad Hatter," Anastasia was shot to death sitting in his barber's chair, one of the most famous mob hits of all time.

YASSIR ARAFAT   The founder of Al Fatah, an underground Palestinian terrorist group, Yassir Arafat became the head of the violent terrorist Palestinian Liberation Organization, founded when the Palestinians lost the Gaza Strip in 1967.

BENEDICT ARNOLD   An American general in the American Revolution, he became a turncoat, offering to deliver West Point to the British for a large sum in sterling. The plot was foiled, and Arnold was given a command in the royal army.

ATILLA THE HUN   In 434 A.D. Atilla became king of the Huns, a group of scattered hordes called the "Scourge of God." A vicious fighter, Atilla invaded all the countries from the Black Sea to the Mediterranean, Gaul, and parts of Italy.

B

BAADER-MEINHOF GANG   An underground radical German terrorist gang, formed in the late 1960s and in existence until the early 1990s, they were responsible for a series of assassinations and bombings that killed over 30 people. Their particular victims were industrialists, bankers, corporate heads, and government officials.

KLAUS BARBIE   The man known as "the butcher of Lyon" where he headed the Fourth Section of the Gestapo. He was responsible for the torture and death of as many as 26,000 people, mainly Jews, and was

awarded the First Class Iron Cross with Swords by Hitler. At the end of World War II, Barbie escaped to South America until he was found and deported to France where he was sentenced to life imprisonment for crimes against humanity. He died in 1991.

BLACK BART   A California stagecoach robber whose real name was Charles E. Boles who struck 28 Wells Fargo stagecoaches from 1875–1883. His trademark clothing was a linen duster and a floursack mask. He carried an unloaded shotgun, but

never hurt a passenger. He was finally tracked down by a Wells Fargo detective, and was sentenced to six years in San Quentin. He died in New York in 1917.

MARK ORRIN BARTON In 1999, a 44-year-old chemist from Atlanta went on a murder spree that left 13 people dead, including himself. First, with a hammer, he bludgeoned to death his wife and two children, an 8-year-old daughter and an 11-year-old son, leaving their bodies in an apartment for days. Then he went into two stock trading offices, and armed with 9mm and .45-caliber handguns, proceeded to kill nine people. Barton had taken up day-trading, and had lost at least $80,000, and this was his idea of payback.

ELIZABETH BATHORY A member of the powerful Hungarian Bathory family, Elizabeth Bathory, born in 1560, became known as the "Bloody Countess" for her murders and obsession with blood. Convinced that blood held the key to the aging process, Bathory tortured and had sex with her serving girls, murdered them, and drank and bathed in their blood. The exact amount of murders is unknown, but it is believed that the number  was somewhere between 50 and several hundred. In 1610 the countess was arrested, tried as a murderer and vampire, and walled up in her room. She was discovered dead four years later by her guards.

DAVID BERKOWITZ   The "Son of Sam" gunman. Before the attacks began in 1975, Berkowitz had been known to the New York City police for having set over a thousand fires in the city, recording each one in a diary. Claiming to be pursued by demons and obsessed by his neighbor Sam's dog, the Son of Sam was responsible for several deaths and shooting assaults with a .44. The manhunt for this serial terrorist went on for two years. Ultimately, Berkowitz confessed that the stories of demons and dogs were invented to set up an insanity plea. He was sentenced to 365 years in prison.

KENNETH BIANCI   Also known as The Hillside Strangler for the series of murders of women left dead on the hillsides of Los Angeles in the late 1970s. With his accomplice, his cousin, Angelo Buono, Bianci was responsible for at least ten deaths, and Bianci alone for another two in Seattle. Both men are currently in prison.

BILLY THE KID   Born Henry McCarty, Billy the Kid was one of the West's most vicious outlaws in the late 1800s, having killed, according to legend, twenty-one men before his twenty-first birthday, using either a Colt revolver or Remington shotgun. Dead before he was 22, Billy spent his entire life on the run from lawmen.

BLACKBEARD THE PIRATE The scourge of the Atlantic Ocean and the Caribbean Sea from 1716 through 1718. British, Blackbeard's real name was Edward Teach. As a young seaman, he served on a British privateer based in Jamaica, allowed by Queene Anne, as privateers were, to plunder French and Spanish ships during the War of the Spanish Succession, and to keep the stolen goods. After the war, Teach became captain of his own ship, added cannons, reinforced the ship's sides, and could carry a crew of 250 pirates. As his power and reputation as the most frightening of pirates grew, so did his beard and hair. He began calling himself Blackbeard, braiding the beard and tying it with black ribbons. He made his base in the Outer Banks of North Carolina, and was ultimately killed by Lieutenant Robert Maynard of the Royal Navy of Ocracoke, the island where Blackbeard had his hideaway.

FRANK BOMPENSIERO This San Diego mobster and hit man specialized in murdering fellow mobsters. One of the most feared men of his era, "The Bomp" became boss of San Diego where he was known for his killings in the frequent mob wars. When associate Jimmy Fratianno found out in 1976 that Bompensiero had become an informant for the FBI, a hit on Bompensiero was ordered, which took six months to execute.

WILLIAM BONIN   Known as the Freeway Killer who, starting in 1978 until his arrest in 1980, raped and murdered 21 teenage boys and young men along the freeways of Orange County, California. He was executed at San Quentin on February 23, 1996.

 **BONNIE AND CLYDE**   Bonnie Parker and Clyde Chestnut Barrow robbed banks and businesses during the Depression, in Texas, Oklahoma, Missouri, Louisiana, and New Mexico—and their robberies often involved shootings and killings. They died in a shootout with police on May 23, 1934, two years after they started their crime spree, a spree that was often applauded by the public since the couple and their entourage were young, good-looking, and dared to thwart authority.

JOHN WILKES BOOTH   A popular actor of his day, he assassinated President Abraham Lincoln at Ford's Theatre in Washington, D.C. on April 14, 1865.

LIZZIE BORDEN   Born in 1860 in Fall River, Massachusetts, she was tried for the ax murders of her father and stepmother in 1892. Claiming she was not home when the murders occurred, she was acquitted. The case has never been solved, and has become the source of numerous books, films, and songs.

LUCRETIA BORGIA Born the illegitimate daughter of Pope Alexander VI at the height of the Italian Renaissance, Lucretia Borgia has often been called the most depraved woman in history. She supposedly disposed of her enemies by pricking them with a poisonous ring.

LOUIS LEPKE BUCHALTER Before being executed at Sing Sing

Prison in Ossining, New York, in March 1944, Buchalter functioned as the head of Murder, Inc., the national crime syndicate's enforcement arm. As many as 100 corpses were attributed to Lepke himself, while those under his control may have slain hundreds more.

TED BUNDY One of the most notorious of all serial killers whose reign of terror across the United States in the 1970s left at last 36 young women mutilated and murdered. When the police finally captured him, in February 1978, he had eluded their chase for more than a year. Bundy was tried three times, beginning in February 1978, with Bundy serving as his own defense lawyer. He received the death penalty by electric chair and was executed on January 24, 1989.

GAIUS CALIGULA   Gaius Caesar Caligula was appointed emperor of Rome after the death of Tiberius in 37 A.D. He squandered the enormous wealth left by Tiberius, and banished and murdered his relatives and competitors. He initiated torture and executions, and was finally assassinated in 41 A.D.

LIEUTENANT WILLIAM L. CALLEY, JR.   In 1968, Calley, commander of Charlie Company of the U.S. troops in Vietnam, ordered an attack on the village of My Lai. When it was discovered that there were no Viet Cong hiding in the village and the villagers were unarmed, the mission was termed a massacre. Calley was convicted of killing at last twenty-two people, and was sentenced to hard labor for life.

THE CAMBRIDGE SPIES   Four very aristocratic Englishmen who all met at Trinity College, Cambridge University in the 1930s, and who were active spies for the Soviet Union for over thirty years. They were the most efficient espionage agents against American and British interests of any spies in the Twentieth Century. They were: Kim Philby, who has been called the Spy of the Century and served the

KGB for almost fifty years; Donald Maclean, Guy Burgess, and Anthony Blunt.

THOMAS CAPANO Lawyer, millionaire, power broker, one of the most influential men in the state of Delaware, married man and father of four, who murdered Anne Marie Fahey, secretary to the governor of the state and girl friend to Capano, because she wanted to end their illicit affair. It was one of Capano's own brothers who came forward with the truth: Thomas had asked his brother to go on a 'fishing' trip in June 1996 with a rather large fishing cooler. Then another of Thomas Capano's lovers also testified that he had asked her to buy a gun for him before that fateful June. During the investigation and trial, Capano emerged as a decadent, deceitful liar who would probably still be free if not for his brother's guilty conscience about throwing Fahey's body, in the ice chest, overboard. Thomas Capano has been sentenced to death.

AL CAPONE One of the first and most influential heads of organized crime in America. After taking over as Chicago boss, he controlled bootlegging, gambling, brothels, and other illegal industries in his territories in the 1920s. He readily murdered his competition, the most famous episode being the St Valentine's Day massacre in 1929. Al Capone spent many years as Public Enemy #1. Federal agent Elliot Ness tried to get him

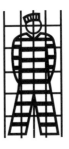

for years, finally succeeding in arresting him for federal tax evasion. Capone was fined $80,000 and served most of an 11-year sentence in Alcatraz. He died in 1947 at the age of 48.

CARLOS THE JACKAL   Carlos was born in Caracas, Venezuela in 1949, and named Ilich Ramirez Sanchez. As "Carlos the Jackal," he became one of the world's most notorious terrorists for hire. He was supposedly tied to the 1975 seizure of an OPEC oil minister, the

1976 hijacking of an Air France jet to Uganda, even the terrorist events at the 1972 Olympics. Eluding arrest for years, he was finally captured in 1994, found guilty of many terrorist events, and held in a French prison where he remains.

ROBERT CHAMBERS   The Preppie Murderer. On a morning in August 1986, the body of Jennifer Levin–a lovely, young girl–was found in New York City's Central Park, discovered to have been killed by Robert Chambers during an episode of rough sex in the park. The Preppie Murder trial was notorious for putting the victim on trial since Levin had been known to chase after Chambers even when he had no interest in her. Chambers, however, was sentenced to prison. He remains there, consistently denied parole, and often in solitary confinement for continued drug use.

WHITTAKER CHAMBERS A journalist and editor for *Time* magazine in the 1940s, and a former member of the American Communist Party who condemned Alger Hiss, a high level counsel to the State Department and an adviser at the Yalta  Conference, to infamy when he testified that Hiss was also a Communist and a spy on behalf of the Soviet Union. Despite his denials, Hiss went to prison for 44 months for perjury, and was ultimately vindicated of spy charges, yet the case remains questionable and famous, not in the least because it reflected the terrors driven by the so-called Red Menace and a young representative named Richard Nixon's zeal in prosecuting Hiss.

 **MARK DAVID CHAPMAN** On December 8, 1980, as Beatles star John Lennon and his wife Yoko Ono approached their New York City apartment building, the Dakota, Lennon was shot and killed at close range. The killer, a deranged 25-year-old security guard from Hawaii named Mark David Chapman had earlier in the day obtained Lennon's signature on a new record album. Chapman is serving 20 years to life in Attica prison and was denied parole in 2000. He will be eligible again in 2002.

JOHN CHRISTIE The famous murderer of 10 Rillington Place in London. A postman with an affinity for violence and prostitutes, Christie brought women to his home, had sex with them, and then

murdered them. He also murdered his wife, and left her, like the others, as trophies in the house until the police had reason to investigate. These bodies were buried in cupboards, under floor boards, and in the garden. Christie was hanged in 1953.

ANDREI CHIKATILO In the 1980s, one of the most notorious and barbaric of all serial killers, known as Russia's Hannibal Lecter, guilty of fifty-two murders, primarily of young women and occasionally boys, some as young as seven. Many of his victims were tortured and mutilated, their bodies unrecognizable. Chikatilo was forced to stay in a cage during his trial, and was eventually put to death in 1994.

MARY ANN COTTON Considered Great Britain's worst serial killer. She was hanged after being convicted in 1873 of having used arsenic poison to kill more than twenty victims—her husbands, her own children, and other relatives.

DR. HAWLEY HARVEY CRIPPEN Crippen was a London dentist in the early twentieth century who shot his wife Belle in 1910, after a ten-year affair with Ethel Le Never. Needing to dispose of the body, he chose their cellar and in order to accommodate the small space, he dissected her body, burned her bones, buried most of what remained in the cellar, and disposed of her limbs, head and organs in a canal near his house. Crippen was convicted and executed in November 1910. His body was buried with a photograph and love letters from Ethel.

JUAN CORONA A native Mexican, Corona was a picker in Yuba City, California in the early 1950s. In 1971, in a fruit orchard where he worked, a freshly dug hole turned out to be a grave. Ultimately, 25 corpses were found, all itinerant farm laborers. What linked Corona to the grisly deaths were two receipts with his signature found in one of the graves. Corona was sentenced to 25 consecutive life terms, and is currently in Corcoran State Prison in California.

JEFFREY DAHMER Known as the Milwaukee Cannibal, one of the most notorious serial murderers in history was suspected as a child and teenager of killing and mutilating neighborhood animals. At eighteen, he brought home a nineteen-year-old hitchhiker whom he clubbed and strangled. He then dismembered and mutilated the victim's remains. This pattern of murder followed by dismemberment and mutilation continued until his arrest in 1991 after a 13-year killing spree with close to 20 victims. Dahmer was murdered in prison on November 28, 1994 at the age of 34.

RONALD DEFEO, JR. The oldest of four children who murdered six members of his family in Amityville, New York, shooting each of them as they slept in their beds. Although he came from a comfortable middle-class family and had never wanted for anything, he and his father did not get along, and Butch, as Ronald Jr. was known, had a vicious temper. By the age of 17, his violent outbursts, fueled by heroin and LSD, were becoming psychotic. At the age of 18, he arranged to have himself 'robbed' of some money his father had given him to deposit. A brutal fight ensued with his father, and in the early morning hours of November 14, 1974, Butch selected a rifle from the collection of weapons he owned, went into his parents' bedroom, and shot the first of eight fatal shots he would fire that night. Within seconds, his mother and father were dead. Next came his two young brothers. Amazingly, no one was awakened by the sound of rifle shots. Last were Butch's two sisters. In less than fifteen mintues, he had slain every member of his family. He went to work the next day at a car dealership as usual. Eventually, all the evidence pointed to Butch, and although he tried to plead insanity, the jury saw him as a violent, cold-blooded killer. He was sentenced to twenty-five years to life on all six counts of murder, and remains in a New York State prison, still without any remorse for his actions.

ALBERT DeSALVO   Thirteen single women in the Boston area were victims of either a single serial killer or several killers between June 1962 and January 1964. All had been sexually molested and strangled with articles of clothing in their own apartments. There were no forced entries. Albert DeSalvo, a married man who had a history of breaking and entering and numerous assaults, confessed to being the Boston Strangler, but there were many confusing issues, including the inadmissibility of his confession and the defense plea of insanity. Finally, in January 1967, DeSalvo was tried on charges of being the "Green Man," another serial killer. Four of the victims testified at the trial. DeSalvo was convicted and sentenced to life imprisonment. In November 1973, DeSalvo was stabbed to death at Walpole State Prison.

NGO DINH DIEM   Vietnamese political leader who served as president, with dictatorial powers, of South Vietnam from 1955 until his assassination in 1963. He abolished free elections; established an autocratic regime staffed by members of his own family; imprisoned and killed hundreds of Buddhists since he preferred fellow Roman Catholics; and left his countrymen in poverty while he grew richer. Loudly anti-Communist, his cruelty and subsequent unpopularity with his people allowed the Communist influence to grow in the South, and inspired the National Liberation Front, or Viet Cong, which launched an increasingly intense guerrila war against his government. Diem's own generals assassinated him during a coup d'état in 1963.

John Dillinger   Born bad and grew up worse. While still in high school, his favorite role model was Jesse James, the frontier outlaw. While serving a ten to twenty year sentence for assault, Dillinger fell in with a group of convicts who taught him  the ropes about bank robbing, and the minute Dillinger was paroled for good behavior, his rampage in the mid-1930s began. A young agent with the Chicago office of the FBI, Melvin Purvis, made capturing Public Enemy #1 and his gang his personal crusade. On a Sunday in July, 1934, the FBI shot him outside a movie theater in Chicago—thanks to a woman betraying him to the enemy.

Emperor Domitian Of Rome   One of the insane emperors of Rome who ruled at about 80 AD. His cruelty was legendary, supposedly having invented a new method of torture which involved burning the sexual organs of his victims. He had all Jews tracked

down and killed. He had three Vestal Virgins executed on grounds of immorality and had the Chief Vestal buried alive. He was ultimately killed by being hacked to death.

DIANE DOWNS A vicious sociopath who killed her oldest child and tried to murder her other two children, claiming that they were shot during an attempted carjacking on a deserted road in Springfield, Oregon. She shot the children to get rid of them because they were an obstacle in a love affair. She escaped once from prison, and is now serving life plus 50 years, and her story was made into a bestselling book and television miniseries, *Small Sacrifices*.

MARTIN DUMMOLARD A mass murderer in France at the end of the nineteenth century, Dummolard and his girlfriend, Justine Lafayette, murdered about eighty young girls. Both were necrophiles, and together they drank the blood of the victims and also ate body parts. The two "vampires" were put on trial; Justine was guillotined and Dummolard confined to an asylum, where he died early in the twentieth century.

"PAPA DOC" DUVALIER Up to 60,000 Haitians died during the 1957-1971 reign of Duvalier, and millions were exiled. He created one of the most feared group

of henchmen, the Tontons Macoutes who terrorized and murdered his political foes as well as ordinary citizens. Trained as a doctor, Duvalier declared himself President-for-Life in 1964, and portrayed himself as a semi-divine, voodoo-empowered ruler. After his death, his son "Baby Doc" was enthroned, and carried on his father's vicious policies until he was driven out of the country in 1986. As a result of Papa Doc's corrupt policies which spawned a fabulously wealthy elite and a dirt-poor populace, Haiti is considered one, if not the, poorest nation in the world.

FELIKS DZERZHINSKII   The founder of the first Russian secret police, called the Cheka, established in 1917. The Cheka was the most feared institution, and played a huge role in the Russian revolution as an instrument of Josef Stalin's brutality against his own countrymen. The Cheka, which eventually became the KGB, established the gulag labor camps in Siberia. Dzerzhinskii was shot in 1953, by Premier Malenkov after Stalin's death.

ADOLF EICHMANN   The head of the Gestapo Department for Jewish Affairs for Hitler, responsible for keeping the trains rolling from all over Europe to the death camps. After the war, with the help of the SS underground, he escaped to Argentina where he lived under an assumed name until 1960 when Israeli Mossad agents brought him back to Jerusalem to stand trial. He was found guilty and hanged at Ramleh Prison in 1962.

COLIN FERGUSON   On December 6, 1993, he went on a shooting rampage on a Long Island, New York, railroad car, killing six passengers and injuring 19. Although a "black rage" defense was tried by defense specialist William M. Kunstler, Ferguson fired him and chose to defend himself. He was found guilty and sentenced to six consecutive life sentences, which is about 200 years of prison time.

CHARLES "PRETTY BOY" FLOYD   Floyd was one of the most colorful bank robbers in America's Depression era. Though a trigger-fingered outlaw, he modeled himself after the desperados of the Wild West and was often seen as a Robin Hood who enjoyed hitting back against the wealthy. He became associated with other outlaws of the time, including Dillinger, Bonnie and Clyde, and "Baby Face" Nelson. Pursued by J. Edgar Hoover's FBI, Floyd was unwittingly involved in the Kansas City Massacre in 1933, in which police and FBI agents were killed. Although Floyd denied involvement in the massacre, he was pursued and when agents caught up with him in 1934 in Ohio, he was gunned down.

Francisco Franco   A cunning politician and fascist, Franco ruled  Spain with an iron fist from 1936 until his death in 1975. Born in northwest Spain in 1892, Franco took power during the Spanish Civil War, and was appointed head of state and Generalissimo of the army in 1936. He was a ruthless ruler and ordered Spain purged of Loyalist supporters and hundreds of thousands were either executed or imprisoned.

Hans Frank   Nazi lawyer and leader of occupied Poland, Frank earned the nickname of the "Jew Butcher of Cracow." Under his rule, nearly all Polish Jews were exterminated, and the nation of Poland disappeared as a national entity with the murder of Poland's leaders, educated elite, and clergy. At the Nuremberg trial Frank was sentenced to death by hanging.

Lynette "Squeaky" Fromme   Fromme was part of the Charles Manson family, and was involved in an attempted assassination of President Gerald Ford.

G

JOHN WAYNE GACY   The "Killer Clown" was a popular businessman in Des Plaines, Illinois, known for performing as a clown at local hospitals. Beginning in 1972, Gacy raped, tortured, and murdered 31 young men. Most of the bodies were discovered in a crawl space under his house. When others were discovered in the Des Plaines and Illinois Rivers, Gacy explained that he had run out of room on his property. Gacy was eventually put to death by lethal injection.

ED GEIN   The inspiration for the serial killer in *The Silence of the Lambs*, as well as for Norman Bates in *Psycho*, Ed Gein treasured women's skin and wore it like clothing. He killed so many young girls during the 1940s and 1950s in Wisconsin—as well as robbed graves to get the skulls and bones he liked to live with—that no tally was ever reached. He was declared guilty by reason of insanity at his trial and was incarcerated in an asylum until his death in 1984.

GARY GILMORE On January 17, 1977, Gary Gilmore was executed by firing squad in Utah State prison. In July 1976, on parole from a twelve-year sentence for armed robbery, Gilmore had murdered a motel owner and a gas attendant before he was captured. Norman Mailer's *The Executioner's Song* is based on the Gilmore case.

HERMANN GOERING As Commander-in-Chief of the Luftwaffe, President of the Reichstag, and Prime Minister of Prussia, Goering was the designated successor to Hitler. In 1933 Goering created the secret state police, the Gestapo, and later initiated preparations for the Wannsee Conference where the "solution to the Jewish question" was the main topic. Goering committed suicide in 1946.

JULIO GONZALEZ A Cuban Army deserter and ex-convict who had come to America. He had recently lost his job at a lamp factory in Queens, New York and was reduced to hustling on the streets of the South Bronx. The *Happy Land* bar, an after-hours club that he frequented, was filled to capacity at 2:30 a.m. on Sunday, March 25, 1990. Gonzalez was talking with his ex-girlfriend who worked at the club and refused Gonzalez's demands to get back with him. They argued, he grabbed her, and a bouncer had to throw him out in the street. Gonzalez was enraged. He went to a nearby gas station and found an empty one-gallon container which he filled with gas. Later, at around 3:30 in the morning, he walked back to the *Happy Land Club*, and dumped the gasoline on the floor and steps of the hallway. Then he lit two matches and threw them onto the floor. The entire place ignited. Ultimately, the *Happy Land* fire, started by a man who had no job, no prospects; whose girl had dumped him; and who was drunk on cheap beer, caused the deaths of 87 people.

 **JOHN GOTTI** Known as the "Dapper Don" because of his elegant style of dress, he became the head of New York's Gambino crime family when he master-minded the Sparks restaurant massacre of would-be Gambino successor, Paul Castellano, in 1985. It took the government until 1992 to convict Gotti, and only then because his colleague, Sammy "the Bull" Gravano, turned informant and ratted him out.

H

FRITZ HAARMANN On May 17, 1924, children playing at the edge of a river in a park in Hannover, Germany, found a human skull. Several days later, more skulls were found and autopsies revealed them to be from 22 teenagers and young people. Every thief and sexual deviant was questioned, and Fritz Haarmann, a clothing and meat salesman known as a homosexual and sex offender, emerged as the suspect. During questioning, Haarmann, who was called the "Butcher of Hannover," broke down and confessed. Haarmann was decapitated in Hannover prison.

JOHN HAIGH   One of the most gruesome murderers, also called the "acid bath vampire" after claiming to drink the blood of the six victims he disposed of in vats of acid. A British forger and fraudster, Haigh would befriend his victims, then kill them, and then fake legal documents to secure their money and goods after their death. Although he tried to plead insanity, it didn't work, and he was convicted and hanged in 1949.

ERIC HARRIS AND DYLAN KLEBOLD   The two teenagers responsible for the massacre at Columbine High School in Littleton, Colorado in April 1999, where 15 people were killed, including themselves.

JEAN HARRIS   The girls' school headmistress who shot and killed her lover in a fit of rage in 1980. Cardiologist Dr. Herman Tarnower, author of the hugely popular Scarsdale Diet, had been Harris's lover for several years, but wanted now to break it off. Harris, jealous and furious, shot him four times in his home in Scarsdale, New York. She was sentenced to prison, and released in the mid-1990s.

BRUNO HAUPTMANN The man who kidnapped Charles Lindbergh's baby in 1934—known as the Crime of the Century. Hauptmann was executed by electric chair in 1936.

GEORGE JO HENNARD In 1991, Hennard, who hated women, crashed his Ford Ranger into the plate glass window of a restaurant in Killeen, Texas. Using a pair of 9mm handguns, the one-time cement worker and merchant marine shot to death 22 people—mostly women—before turning the guns on himself. It is the deadliest mass shooting in the history of the United States.

RUDOLF HESS Formerly the number three man in Hitler's Germany, Hess fled to England on 1941, where he attempted to negotiate peace with the British, who promptly imprisoned him for the duration of the war. Found guilty at the Nuremberg trial, Hess was sentenced to life imprisonment. Hess was the sole surviving Nazi and the only inmate in Spandau prison until 1987, when he committed suicide at age 92.

RICHARD HICKOCK With Perry Smith, they massacred the Clutter family in Kansas in 1959, and this became the basis of Truman Capote's *In Cold Blood*. Smith and Hickock had met in prison; they were both petty thieves who killed Herbert Clutter, his wife and two children for an alleged $5000 they had heard was kept in a safe. The two got all of $50 and a portable radio. Hickock and Smith were hanged in 1968, and *In Cold Blood* revolutionized journalism.

HENRICH HIMMLER After joining the Nazi party in 1925, Heinrich Himmler was the director of propaganda and head of the SS before assuming control of the Gestapo in 1934. He exercised overall control of Hitler's concentration camps and the "Final Solution" to the "Jewish problem" during World War II, including Auschwitz as the main extermination center. Himmler poisoned himself after capture by the British in 1945.

JOHN HINCKLEY In 1981 in Washington, D.C., the 25-year-old tried to assassinate President Ronald Reagan. He also seriously wounded

James S. Brady, Reagan's press secretary, and this led to a nationwide effort to change gun control laws. Hinckley was obsessed with the actress Jodie Foster and thought she would be impressed if he assassinated Reagan.

EMPEROR HIROHITO   This Japanese monarch, who became emperor in 1926, ordered the bombing of Pearl Harbor as an ally of the Axis powers in World War II.

ADOLF HITLER   The most hated figure of the twentieth century, Hitler was made dictator of Germany in 1933. A believer in the superiority of the Aryan race, he prepared his nation for war, embarked on the conquest of Europe, and initiated a "Final Solution" to the "Jewish prob-lem." Hitler was responsible for the institution of the "concentration camp" where civilian victims were tortured, shot, starved, and gassed to death. The final death toll under his regime was 11 million. Hitler committed suicide in his bunker as Berlin fell to the Allies. Hitler remains the incarnation of absolute evil.

JAMES OLIVER HUBERTY   In July 1984, welder, former apprentice undertaker, and unemployed security guard Huberty walked through the door of a McDonald's restaurant in San Ysidro, California, announced he was "hunting humans" and proceeded to unpack a 12-gauge pump shotgun, a 9mm pistol, and a 9mm semiautomatic carbine. He killed 21 people before being shot to death by a police sharpshooter.

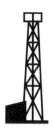

SADDAM HUSSEIN Born in 1937 and a key member of the Arab nationalist movement, Saddam Hussein became President of Iraq in 1979 and solidified his dictatorship by nationalizing the country's oil industry. In 1990, Hussein invaded Kuwait leading to the Gulf War. He is a fanatic enemy of the United States.

JUDAS ISCARIOT The apostle who betrayed Jesus Christ—for money. The name Judas has become synonomous with treachery.

IVAN THE TERRIBLE Ivan IV Vasilyevich was the first Russian ruler to be formally crowned as czar in 1547. Although he did much to reform and expand Russia, he was also known for his erratic and despotic power over his entire domain. In 1570 he ravaged the town of Novgorod and ordered the slaying of hundreds of its inhabitants after hearing rumors of conspiracy. In 1580, he struck and killed his eldest and favorite son.

J

JACK THE RIPPER   This never-captured English murderer killed and mutilated five London prostitutes between August and November 1888. The case file was closed in 1892, but speculation about his identity continues to this day.

JESSE JAMES   A ruthless bank and train robber, before he died at the age of 34, Jesse James had committed dozens of robberies and killed

at least six men. He assumed the role of avenger for the post-Civil War South, rampaging against the North and its wealth. To many, he became a folklore hero who fought on behalf of farm workers against industrialization.

JIM JONES   The Reverend Jim Jones, who led the People's Temple in San Francisco and moved it to Jonestown, Guyana, ordered more than 900 followers to drink cyanide-laced grape punch. The mass suicide occurred on November 18, 1978, and Jim Jones was found dead with a bullet wound in the head.

WINNIE RUTH JUDD In one of the most notorious cases in the annals of American crime, Winnie Ruth Judd, "The Trunk Murderess" was convicted of murder when she was 26 years old. Judd was the wife of a physician thirty years her senior. In the summer of 1931, he left for Los

Angeles where he was seeking a job in a clinic, and he left Winnie Ruth behind in their home in Phoenix. She began an affair with Jack Halloran, a prosperous lumber yard owner who was married. On Friday, October 16, 1931, Winnie Ruth spent the night with her two girlfriends, and an argument broke out. During or after the fight, the two women were shot to death. Winnie Ruth would claim they were killed in self-defense during a struggle. With Halloran's help, the body of one of the young women was put into a trunk. The other body had to be dismembered to fit into another trunk. Winnie Ruth returned to her job as a receptionist the next day, and also removed some of the body parts from one of the trunks to reduce its weight, putting them in a valise. She had the trunks put on a train and made the 400-mile trip to Los Angeles with the valise at her side. When the

train arrived at Union Station, the baggage handler was overcome with nausea from the stench in the trunks. He noticed a liquid oozing that appeared to be blood. Winnie disappeared, only to be found four days later. She was tried for murder, found guilty, and sentenced to death by hanging. While awaiting execution, she had a sanity hearing and was pronounced insane. She was moved to a state hospital. The death sentence was ultimately commuted to life imprisonment. From 1939 to 1962, she escaped five times, the last time maintaining a life for herself for six and a half years as a maid and companion to a wealthy doctor and his wife in Northern California, before being taken into custody again. In 1971, Winnie Ruth Judd was released after 40 years of confinement, the most of any female in an American prison. She died in 1998 at the age of 93, in Phoenix.

THEODORE KACZYNSKI The socially withdrawn math prodigy turned recluse spent almost 20 years sending letter bombs to members of academia and the technology industry. In 1996, the FBI finally arrested the Unabomber after his brother turned him in. He is serving consecutive life sentences.

ALVIN KARPIS A Depression era desperado who became Public Enemy #1, eluded capture by the FBI for five years while committing bank robberies, kidnappings, and murders. Karpis was the only man J. Edgar Hoover ever arrested as Director of the FBI, and Karpis went

on to spent more than 26 years on Alcatraz, more time in that prison than any other man.

ANDREW KEHOE Born in 1872, he was one of thirteen children who was raised in Tecumseh, Michigan, near East Lansing. He married a wealthy young woman he met in college and they bought a large farm outside the village of Bath, where he was elected to the school board in 1926. Kehoe absolutely loathed paying taxes, and for no reason, blamed the Bath Consolidated School for his financial troubles, his wife's illness, anything and everything. Kehoe worked as the Bath Consolidated School handyman since he was mechanically very adept. During the winter of 1926, Kehoe began to accumulate explosives and began an extensive wiring set-up in the school. He also rigged a series of fire bombs in every structure of his farm and in his home. On May 17, 1927, Kehoe killed his ill wife by bashing in her skull. On May 18, 1927, there were over 1,000 pounds of dynamite waiting for the school children and teachers to arrive at Bath Consolidated School. By nine o'clock in the morning, Kehoe had detonated all the bombs on his farm, destroying it completely, and had set off the bombs at the school, as well as a bomb attached to the truck he was driving.

Hundreds of people were wounded; dozens were killed at the school, including more children than at any other incident of school violence in the history of the United States. Kehoe was killed in his truck. A madman who picked an innocent target—and obliterated it, making him and the crime one of the worst in history.

GEORGE R. KELLY   Another of the Midwest criminals sought along with Bonnie and Clyde and John Dillinger was "Machine Gun Kelly." Kelly's short and colorful career was highlighted by one of the most daring kidnappings in United States history. In July of 1933, Kelley walked up to a mansion owned by oil tycoon Charles F. Urschel of Oklahoma City, interrupted a bridge game, and under threat of a tommy gun ordered both men in the game into a car. When Urschel was identified, his bridge partner was let go and Urschel was brought to Texas and held for $200,000 ransom. After the ransom was received, the victim was left 20 miles outside Oklahoma City. With the FBI on Kelly's heels, he was chased and finally arrested in Memphis, Tennessee. He was extradited to Oklahoma City, tried, and sentenced to life in Leavenworth.

DR. JACK KEVORKIAN   Also known as Dr. Death for his role in assisting the 'suicides' of seriously ill people who had lost the ability to live on their own and wanted to die. He believes that people have the right to avoid a lingering, miserable death, and they should have dignity in death as in life. For almost ten years and close to 50 assisted suicides, Kevorkian avoided legal penalties, but in 1998, he crossed from passive to active euthanasia when he gave a man a lethal injection, rather than providing the patient, as he had done in the past, with the means to kill himself. Kevorkian videotaped the act for broadcast on national television, daring prosecutors to charge him with murder. They did, and in early 1999, Kevorkian was found guilty and sentenced to 10 to 25 years in prison.

AYATOLLAH RUHOLLAH KHOMEINI This Islamic fundamentalist who considered the United States the embodiment of Satan, was exiled from Iran in 1964 for criticizing the Shah. In 1979 he returned to Iran and held power until his death in 1989. The Ayatollah's stance was extreme, and the losses in the long war he waged with Iraq were matched by the thousands who died in his prisons.

KIP KINKEL On May 20, 1998, this 15-year-old high school student walked through the cafeteria of his suburban Oregon high school, opening fire with a semi-automatic rifle, killing two students, wounding 20 more, and this was after he had murdered his parents, shooting them at home. The house was rigged with several deadly explosive traps in the hope of causing further harm. He is serving 111 years in prison.

DAVID KORESH A charismatic leader of the Branch Davidian cult, he would not give himself or his group up to the FBI, and on April 19, 1993, Koresh, and 80 followers, including 18 children, died by fire or gunfire after FBI agents surrounded their compound outside Waco, Texas. The deaths were called a mass suicide and followed more than 50 days of an armed standoff.

RANDY KRAFT The "Southern California Strangler" operated at the same time and area as the "Freeway Killer" William Bonin—and was often confused with him. The signatures of his killings involved tor-

ture and mutilation of his young male victims. The first bodies were found in 1972 and after a rash of murders, they slowed down by 1977, leading police to think they might not be related. In 1978, however, the murders began again and by December 1979 there were 14 new victims. Finally, Kraft was arrested and convicted of murdering 16 people although the tally may have been up to 42. He awaits execution on Death Row.

KRAY TWINS   Born on the outskirts of London in 1933, Ronnie and Reggie Kray grew up to be England's most infamous gangsters. Cockney villains, they built a criminal network of drug dealing, union corruption and terrorism. By 1956, they controlled a large area of London and collected dues from criminals, pubs, and gambling establishments. The twins spent time in jail and in psychiatric prisons. They were finally convicted of the murders of two street thugs.

PETER KURTEN   The "Vampire of Dusseldorf" was responsible for murdering or assaulting 29 people during his reign of terror in the German city in the late 1880s. His first attack was thought to have occurred in 1892 and continued for more than thirty years. His victims were strangled and raped, after which he slit their throats and drank their blood. He was killed by guillotine in 1931. The movie *M* was inspired by his story.

L

JEAN LAFITTE   Smuggler, privateer, pirate, and slaver who was ultimately pardoned when he helped defend New Orleans from British attack during the War of 1812. Still, he remains one of the most notorious pirates in history.

NATHAN LEOPOLD AND RICHARD LOEB   The infamous college boys who, in 1924 in a suburb of Chicago, kidnapped and murdered a young boy because they were bored and wanted to create the 'perfect crime' to outsmart everyone else. The famous Clarence Darrow handled the defense for the boys who ultimately confessed. Darrow was interested in sparing their lives from execution, and he succeeded. They were sentenced to life in prison.

JOHN LIST   Thanks to an airing of the television show *America's Most Wanted* in 1989, the man who in 1971 slaughtered his wife, daughter, mother, and two sons, and left them to rot in their New Jersey home, was finally captured and brought to justice by a former neighbor who knew him as Robert Clark, the nice church-going man married to a woman named Delores. The resemblance nagged at her just enough to call the show. Ultimately, List was proven sane at the time of the murders and sentenced to five consecutive life sentences.

HENRY LEE LUCAS   Born in 1936 in the Virginia back-woods, Lucas had a brutal childhood that turned him into a bitter person. He spent his teen years in and out of jail, escaping and being rearrested. In 1960, after drinking with his mother in a local bar, they had a fight, and he ended up stabbing her to death. He was sentenced to ten years. Paroled in 1970, he became a drifter with a life of crime. When arrested in 1983 on a weapons charge, he told the judge he had murdered 100 women. He was tried and sentenced to 75 years. Lucas then became the focus of other unsolved crimes. After the trial he confessed to murders all over the country, involving bizarre details including dismemberment, necrophila, and cannibalism. Lucas was finally sent to death row, but in 1998, Texas Governor George Bush commuted Lucas' death sentence to life imprisonment because of lack of definitive proof.

LUCKY LUCIANO   Charles Luciano was born in 1897 in Sicily in a town near Palermo and was brought to New York by his parents in 1906. Luciano's childhood in New York was one of crime, his first arrest coming in 1907 for shoplifting. During the same year he began a racket, offering "protection" to smaller kids for a fee. By 1916, "Lucky" Luciano was a leading member of the notorious Five Points Gang and a suspect in several murders. By 1920, he was a power in the bootlegging rackets and was affiliated with several Italian and Jewish gangsters. At the age of 38, Luciano was arrested, tried on several charges, and given 30 to 50 years in prison. Luciano's

sentence was commuted in 1946 with the condition that he be deported to Sicily. Luciano continued his operations from Sicily until he died of a heart attack in 1962. The deportation was lifted so that he could be buried in New York City.

DR. JEFFREY MACDONALD The former Green Beret captain who butchered his pregnant wife and their two daughters, aged 5 and 2, on February 17, 1970 at Ft. Bragg, North Carolina where MacDonald was a group surgeon. To this day, he claims he is innocent, but all appeals for a new trial have been denied. This case was the basis for the huge bestseller, *Fatal Vision*.

NICCOLO MACHIAVELLI The Italian statesman and political philosopher best known for his work *The Prince* written in 1513 in which he puts forth advice designed to keep a ruler in power, advice that is used to this day by businessmen and politicians. The adjective "Machiavellian" has come to describe someone who manipulates others in an opportunistic and duplicitous way.

MARY MALLON "Typhoid Mary," a dishwasher in New York City at the turn of the twentieth century, was thought to have passed typhoid fever to about 1,300 people, changing her name from job to job before she was finally arrested in 1906. She died in government-forced isolation in 1929.

CHARLES MANSON In the summer of 1969, a cult of Manson disciples murdered seven people, including actress Sharon Tate, who was more than eight months pregnant. Their blood was used to write messages on the walls. Manson, an ex-convict and would-be musician had gathered a group of rag-tag losers around him, and convinced them to commit the atrocious crimes. His name has become synonomous with evil. He exists in a top security cell at Corcoran State Prison in California, with no chance for parole.

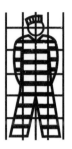

MAO TSE-TUNG Founder of the Chinese Communist Party, Mao achieved the unification of China under a controversial rule that included driving the Chinese nationalists out of the mainland during the Civil War of 1946–49. He created the "Red Guard," a military group formed from students, in order to quell insurrection.

FERDINAND MARCOS The corrupt president of the Philippines from 1966 to 1986. Convicted early in his life for murdering an opponent to his political father, Marcos, a lawyer, eventually got acquitted and began his own political career that lasted until his death in 1989. His authoritarian regime was known for corruption, and for the suppression of all opposition. He and his wife, former beauty queen Imelda Marcos, were charged by the United States with racketeering for embezzling billions of dollars. Imelda was brought to trial after Ferdinand's death, acquitted, and sent back to her country where she was tried and found guilty.

MATA HARI (Margaretha Gertuida Zelle) Born in the Netherlands in 1876, Margaretha Gertrude MacLeod, née Zelle, became a dancer in France in 1905. She had many lovers, several in high military and governmental positions on both sides during World War I. Accused as a spy for the Germans, she was shot in Paris.

JOSEPH McCARTHY Wisconsin's senator from 1947 to 1957, McCarthy won notoriety by charging that the U.S. State Department had been infiltrated by Communists. The 1950s became known as the "McCarthy era," during which he used the infamous House of Representatives Committee on Un-American Activities to hurl accusations and charge disloyalty among prominent people. This created a "communist" scare that ruined the reputations and lives of many Americans, especially scientists, entertainers, artists, and writers.

TIMOTHY MCVEIGH   On April 19, 1995, the
Federal building in Oklahoma City was bombed,
killing 168 people and injuring more than 500
more. It is considered the worst terrorist attack in
American history, and it was masterminded by this
man. Twenty-seven at the time of the Oklahoma
City bombing, McVeigh was an angry young man,
violently anti-government, an ardent survivalist who
had been making and exploding bombs for years.

MENENDEZ BROTHERS   Lyle and Erik Menendez, the sons of a
wealthy Cuban-American executive in Los Angeles, shot their parents
in their Beverly Hills home in 1989. For almost a year, the brothers
went on a spending spree, cashing in on their parents' $13 million
fortune, until the police had enough evidence to suspect and then

arrest them. They confessed, and blamed the shooting
on years of sexual abuse. Their first trial in 1993
ended in a mistrial. In 1996 they were convicted of
first-degree murder and are serving life prison terms
without parole in two different facilities in California.

DR. JOSEPH MENGELE   Medical officer with
the Waffen SS during World War II and chief
doctor at the Auschwitz concentration camp.
He is remembered as the "Angel of Death" for

his grotesque medical experiments performed on Auschwitz inmates. He escaped after the war, supposedly lived in South America, and was never found, although there have been claims he died in the mid-1990s.

VALERIE MESSLINA The third wife of Roman Emperor Claudius, mother of Octavia and Britannicus, instigated a reign of terror that included plots against many of Rome's senators and eventually included her husband. Her name is synonymous with lust and cruelty.

SLOBODAN MILOSEVIC The former president of Yugoslavia who was responsible for the tragic events that brought war to Slovenia, Croatia, Bosnia, and Kosovo, and the ethnic cleansing in the country, particularly between Serbians and Albanians, that has seen mounds of corpses similar to what happened in Europe during Hitler's reign.

BENITO MUSSOLINI Mussolini 's lust for glory proved his downfall, for it linked him with Adolf Hitler. In 1922, after Mussolini led a successful march of Italian Nationalists on Rome, King Vittorio

Emmanuele appointed him Prime Minister, and he assumed a dictatorial role. After his alliance with the Axis and his support of Hitler, as war turned against the Axis, he was dismissed by the King. Mussolini was executed by partisans in 1945.

BABY FACE NELSON   Born in Chicago's southwest side near the Stockyards in 1908, Lester Joseph Gillis grew up to be only five feet four inches, but as Baby Face Nelson, he was one of the toughest Depression-era gangsters. During prohibition, he  became an enforcer for Al Capone, but was let go for too much violence. He killed not just to protect himself, but because he liked killing. Nelson turned to a successful robbery career. After months of chase, FBI agents caught up with him in September 1934. Nelson died in the shootout; he was only 26.

NERO   Emperor Nero, whose mother committed murder in order to get him named the leader of Rome, murdered her for her intrigues and then, when fire destroyed half of Rome, blamed the Christian population and had them rounded up, crucified, and burned alive.

CHARLES NG   In July 1984, this son of a wealthy Hong Kong businessmen, went on a murder spree that included abducting a dozen women and abusing them as sex slaves before brutally killing them all in a rundown mountain cabin in California. He came to the United States at the age of 18, dropping out of college after one semester. With a history of shoplifting and stealing, crime was in his blood, eventually ending up, after joining the Marines and being caught stealing grenade launchers, in the military prison at Fort Leavenworth. He was released in 1984, and the spree began soon after, with a friend, Leonard Lake. Ng became a fugitive after the police got to Lake, and in 1991, was finally extradited from Canada. In 1999, he was sentenced to death. Ng's cold-blooded evil, the joy he killed in torturing his victims makes him one of America's most horrific murderers.

MANUEL NORIEGA   Commander of the National Defense Forces of Panama, he ousted the civilian president, and made himself leader. He has been implicated in drug trafficking, the sale of U.S. secrets to Cuba and Russia while in the pay of the U.S. Army and CIA, and other illegal activities. In 1989, the U.S. invaded Panama, captured Noriega, and brought him to Miami, Florida, where he remains in prison, convicted on racketeering and conspiracy charges.

O

DION O'BANION   An Irish bootlegger and gangster in 1920s Chicago who was a florist by day, and responsible for at least 25 gangland-related murders when he wasn't smelling orchids. He usually wore three guns at a time in suits with specially-made hidden pockets. He became the model for all the James Cagney gangster portrayals in the movies.

LEE HARVEY OSWALD   The assassin who shot President John F. Kennedy on November 22, 1963, from the Texas School Book Depository building in Dallas.

P

POL POT   The Secretary General of what became Cambodia's Khymer Rouge, a popular guerilla force. Having defeated the American-backed Phnom-Penh regime in 1975, Pol Pot began a reign of terror that lasted until 1979, during which 1.7 million people died from starvation and brutality.

GABRILO PRINCIP When this 19-year-old Serbian student assassinated Archduke Francis Ferdinand in Sarajevo in 1914, World War I began.

MOHMMAR QADAFFI A rabid proponent of Middle East supremacy and one of the world's worst terrorists, Colonel Qadaffi, who, at 27, seized the Royal Palace of Libya and overthrew the resident government, was the financier of the "Black September Movement" which perpetrated the 1972 Munich Olympic massacre, as well as numerous other horrific events.

WILLIAM C. QUANTRILL Leader of the Raiders, a guerilla group of pro-slavery sympathizers, mainly from Missouri, who, in 1862, went on looting raids through eastern Kansas. In 1863, he led his 300 followers in a violent attack on Lawrence, Kansas, burning the major buildings and killing between 150 and 200 of the male population.

 **GRIGORI YEFIMOVICH RASPUTIN**   This Russian monk, who gained influence in 1907 over the Tsarina Alexandra of Russia, was probably responsible for the fall of Nicholas II, the last tsar of Russia. He exploited what has been considered his hypnotic power over the Tsarina to ruin the royal family with scandal and create dissent within the Russian court. He was ultimately assassinated by a group of monarchists, after several prior attempts to kill him, including poisoning him, failed.

JAMES EARL RAY   Assassinated Dr. Martin Luther King Jr. on April 4, 1968 in Memphis, Tennessee. He was sentenced to a 99-year prison sentence, and died in jail in 1998 at the age of 70. A small-time criminal, many people believed he was part of a much larger, racist conspiracy, and happened to be the one who pulled the trigger.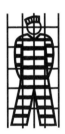

RED BRIGADE   Formed in 1969, this Italian terrorist group sought to separate Italy from the Western Alliance through the assassination and kidnapping of Italian government and business leaders, and was guilty of murdering former Prime Minister Aldo Moro in 1978.

KING RICHARD III The last Plantagenet ruler of England accused of locking away his two young nephews in the Tower of London, and then having them murdered to allow the line of succession to come to him.

MAXIMILIEN ROBESPIERRE Although not the actual inventor of France's "Reign of Terror" after the Revolution, Robespierre was considered a fanatical leader of the Jacobins, who believed that all opponents to the revolution should be beheaded. By 1794 the executions became so intense that a warrant went out for his arrest. He and several of his followers were executed in July 1794.

MARQUIS DE SADE A French nobleman in the mid-eighteenth century who believed that sexual deviation and criminal acts were natural parts of the human life. He spent 27 of his 74 years in prisons and asylums in France, and his name has given rise to the word "sadism" or the pleasure one takes in pain.

SHAKA ZULU   A fierce and militaristic king of the Zulu clan of Africa, he was responsible for the murder of a million people, using the Zulu warriors as he wanted, punishing them mercilessly, usually with death. In 1824, Europeans had arrived, and in a skirmish with an enemy clan, Shaka was stabbed, but treated by the Europeans. They then aided him in his wars to conquer more of South Africa. While on a hunt with the Europeans, word came to Shaka that his beloved mother lay dying. In grief, he ordered several men executed, but in the chaos, 7,000 people died. He then ordered his clan to death by starvation out of reverence to his mother.

On September 22, 1828, Shaka was stabbed to death by his half-brother who took the body and threw it in an empty grain pot, which was then filled with stones. He ruled for 12 years as King Shaka and was 41 years old when he was killed.

PATRICK HENRY SHERRILL   A part-time letter carrier in Edmond, Oklahoma, he walked into the post office there and killed fourteen people before taking his own life, one of the most vicious incidents of post office shootings in the 1980s and 1990s.

THE SHINING PATH An extremist faction of the Peruvian Communist Party and the most radical revolutionary Marxist guerrilla organization in the West today. They are responsible for all sorts of atrocities including torture and murder of captives, massacres of villages, bombings, assassinations; probably close to 12,000 deaths in all.

DR. HAROLD SHIPMAN A general practitioner near Manchester, England, trusted and respected by over 3,000 patients in his lifetime, who was found guilty in 2000, after an arduous two-year investigation, of murdering 15 elderly patients, but responsible for possibly 136 patient deaths. In all but one of the murders, Shipman would visit the patient at home, unannounced, and inject them with a deadly dose of morphine.

O. J. SIMPSON Football player and celebrity, once considered one of the most talented running backs in National Football League history, was accused of the murder of his former wife, Nicole Brown Simpson and her friend Ronald Goodman. Simpson was acquitted of all charges, but in a civil trial in 1997 was found responsible for their deaths.

SIRHAN SIRHAN Assassin of Senator Robert F. Kennedy, presidential hopeful, on June 5, 1968 in Los Angeles.

PAMELA SMART In prison for life without any chance of parole, Smart was convicted of masterminding her husband's murder in their Derry, New Hampshire home on August 1, 1990. Although she did not pull the trigger, she was convicted of telling her 16-year-old lover, William "Billy" Flynn to shoot her husband, which he did with three friends as accomplices; Pamela Smart was twenty-two at the time. Flynn is serving a jail sentence of 28 years to life.

SUSAN SMITH After going on national television to cry for the return of her two young sons in a carjacking in October 1995, Susan Smith confessed to a troubled marriage, a bad affair, consuming isolation and loneliness that compelled her to kill herself and her two boys, but instead turned into murder, by leaving her boys locked in the car, putting it in neutral and letting it roll down into the water while she stood by watching them drown. Susan was sentenced to 30 years to life in prison.

PAUL SNIDER An all-around failure, sleazy pornographer, and obsessively controlling manager and husband of Dorothy Stratton who was

one of *Playboy* magazine's most popular and successful centerfolds and Playmate of the Year. The young, beautiful Stratton had everything ahead of her and was attracting the notice of many of Hollywood's power brokers, including Peter Bogdanovich who had discovered Cybill Shepherd, but the more successful Dorothy became, the more jealous Snider got until he was all-consuming, and he murdered her before turning the shotgun on himself.

RICHARD SPECK   The tattoo on his forearm read "Born to Raise Hell" and Speck did exactly that when he brutally stabbed and murdered eight student nurses in Chicago on July 13, 1966. One survivor, who hid under a bed, was able to identify Speck. The alcoholic, small-time ex-con was sentenced to 50-100 years in prison, but he died from a heart attack in 1991. This remains one of the most horrific butcherings in American history.

JOSEF STALIN   As a student, Stalin became a Marxist revolutionary and in 1922, Lenin appointed him Secretary of the Central Committee of the Communist Party, a post he was to hold for the next 30 years. Before he died in  1924, Lenin had misgivings about his appointment, warning others of Stalin's hunger for power. As Stalin gained control, he brought

charges against older Bolsheviks, purged the Army, collectivized farms—causing starvation—instituted secret police and slave labor, and sought to maintain an empire by imprisoning and/or executing all his opponents. He died in 1953, a hated ruler.

CHARLES STARKWEATHER In 1957, Charles Starkweather, a rebel from Nebraska who modeled himself after James Dean, embarked on a murder spree with his girlfriend Caril Fugate that began with the murder of Caril's disapproving family, included an old family friend, two teenagers, and an industrialist and his wife. Discovered and pur-

sued by the police, Starkweather's final killing was a salesman in Wyoming whose car he tried to hijack. He was convicted and given the death penalty, and was executed in June 1959.

Fugate, because she was 14 years old, received a life sentence. She was paroled in June of 1976.

SUHARTO President of Indonesia from 1967–1998, who unseated former President Sukarno, and a total dictator who suppressed all dissent. Economic instability and popular discontent with his rule forced his resignation in

1998, leaving a legacy of corruption, financial scandal, and military massacres.

PETER SUTCLIFFE   Beginning in 1975 with his first attack, the man known as the "Yorkshire Ripper" waged a 5-year battle of terror against women in England. A loner and victim of bullying, Sutcliffe changed jobs frequently, from a mill, to an engineering apprenticeship, to a factory worker, and then a gravedigger at the Bingley Cemetery in Yorkshire. By the time of his arrest in 1981, he had killed 13 women and left seven others for dead.

T

TAMERLANE   A Turkik Mongol (1336-1405), his goal was to make his capital of Samarkand the most impressive in Asia. Yet he was rarely home, preferring to vanquish and destroy other lands. Legendary for his ruthless savagery and lack of mercy, he massacred entire populations, including the 80,000 residents of Delhi, and razed whole cities, leaving behind nothing but rubble, and rebuilding towers out of the skulls of his victims.

HARRY THAW Millionaire playboy who, in 1906, shot to death Stanford White, one of America's most famous architects. Considered the "crime of the century" before Lindbergh or O.J. Simpson, Thaw's trial had everything: wealth, pedigree, and sex. This was a crime of passion: Stanford White had been having an affair with Thaw's wife, a teenage showgirl, Evelyn Nesbit, also known as "The Girl in the Red Velvet Swing," because gossip had it that White would push a naked Nesbit on a red velvet swing. The notorious case resulted in two trials. The first ended in a hung jury. The second resulted in Thaw being found not guilty by reason of insanity.

TOKYO ROSE Her real name was Iva Ikuko Toguri, but during World War II she was called Tokyo Rose, a 'temptress' who used the radio airwaves to taunt America's fighting

men in the Pacific during the bloody battles there, claiming their defeat at the hands of the Japanese. Ultimately a federal jury convicted her of treason and in 1949, she was sentenced to ten years in prison.

TOMÁS DE TORQUEMADA First General Inquisitor of the Spanish Inquisition, and a man of almost inhuman cruelty, responsible for expelling all Jews from Spain in 1492, for having 8,800 people suffer death by fire, and almost 10,000 others tortured and killed, for the sake of the Inquisition established by Catholic sovereigns.

CLAUS VON BULOW   A Dane who married wealthy
American heiress Martha "Sunny" Crawford in
1966. She had two children from a previous marriage. Sunny and Claus had one daughter. Their
lives were the rich, pampered existences of society,
with homes around the world, particularly
Clarendon Court, a remarkable estate in Newport, Rhode Island. In
1979, von Bulow was given an ultimatum by his mistress, a soap
opera actress, and then that Christmas, Sunny fell into a coma. It was
thought to be a drug overdose, but turned out to be a dangerously low
blood-sugar level. In early December 1980, Sunny was again rushed
to the hospital, having overdosed on aspirin. That Christmas at
Clarendon Court, she fell into another coma, and the efforts to revive
her failed. She was found to have irreversible brain damage, and von
Bulow, still having his affair with the actress, wanted her removed
from life support immediately. Stunned, her two children from her
first marriage hired a private investigator who found a black bag con-
taining hypodermic needles and rugs. Von Bulow was
indicted by a grand jury in July 1981 for twice attempting
to kill his wife by injecting her with insulin. The 1982
trial in Newport was the first ever to be televised live. It
turned out that Sunny had been thinking of divorce
which would have left Claus with some pocket change.
If she died, he stood to inherit $14 million. Von Bulow

was sentenced to 30 years in prison after being found guilty. He hired legal ace Alan Dershowitz to handle his appeal, and in 1984, the verdict was overturned. In 1985, there was a second trial, and he was found not guilty. Sunny has remained in a coma since that night in 1980. Von Bulow lives in London, his daughter Cosima an heir to the fortune. The decadent saga and legal shenanigans were turned into the popular movie, *Reversal of Fortune*.

DR. ALBERT WEINER A successful psychiatrist in the late 1950s, this New Jersey doctor saw up to fifty patients a day. His idea of therapy ranged from powerful muscle relaxants to electric shock treatments. His practice was ended when he was convicted on twelve counts of manslaughter for injecting his patients with unsterilized needles that ultimately caused their deaths.

FRED AND ROSEMARY WEST A couple who lived in Gloucester, England, obsessed with both sexual depravity and death. Once an investigation began, the bodies of twelve victims were found under their house. Fred West was charged with murdering these twelve, which included his first wife and eldest daughter. He committed suicide, but Rose West, convicted in 1995, is serving life in Holloway Prison in north London.

CHARLES WHITMAN   Known
as the Texas Tower Sniper,
Charles Whitman used the 307-foot
University of Texas Tower in Austin to fire
randomly at people below for more than 90 minutes
on August 1, 1966, killing 14 people and injuring dozens
more, before being shot and killed by Austin police officers.

WAYNE WILLIAMS   The Atlanta Child Murderer who killed 27 young
black boys from October 1979 to May 1981, making him a very rare,
African-American serial killer. Williams is serving a life sentence.

AILEEN WUORNOS   The first female serial killer in American history,
a cold-blooded predator who stalked and killed a string of victims
between December 1989 and November 1990. A prostitute, she
claimed she killed in self-defense when cruising the highways of
central Florida, and the men who picked her up got
rough. Rough enough that she killed seven of them.
Although she claimed self-defense, the jury didn't
believe her, and she was sentenced to death in 1992.
She awaits execution on Death Row in Florida.

Z

DIANE ZAMORA   With her boyfriend, David Graham, they murdered Adrianne Jones in what has become known as the Texas Cadet Murder. In 1995, Zamora and Graham were high school lovers in New Braunfels, Texas, who planned to have careers in the military. Graham had sex with Jones, a high school classmate, and he told Diane about it. Her jealousy was so out of control that she told David the only way to repurify their love was to kill Adrianne. The plan was to lure Jones out of her house late at night, which Graham did, with Zamora hiding in the back seat. He drove to a deserted spot; they attacked her, and then Graham shot her to death. They both got life sentences

ZODIAC KILLER   During the late 1960s and early 1970s, the killer known as the "Zodiac," who up to now has eluded capture, terrorized not only the San Francisco Bay area and part of California where he killed, but the entire West Coast. He always killed on weekends or near holidays. He attacked young couples, and was thought to wear a black executioner's hood with a zodiac symbol on the front. He used different weapons, and bragged about his killings, seeking attention by sending the police taunting letters often written in codes and symbols. Although there were only 7 definite victims in this killing spree, Zodiac claimed to have killed 37, and including other unsolved cases, Zodiac may have been responsible for over 50 killings.